INTRODUCTION

Pittenweem derives its name from the Celtic *pit na uaimh*, meaning the 'township of the cave'. This cave is still extant and has long been known as St Fillan's Cave. The oldest recorded spelling of Pittenweem is Petwemokum, which is found in a charter from the reign of King Edgar (1097-1107), dated 1100. In it Edgar granted Pittenweem to the Culdees, a powerful sect of the early Celtic Christian church in Scotland, whose principal foundation was located at Loch Leven. This grant specified that the superiority of Pittenweem and other Culdee property was to be held by the Priory Church of St Andrews. According to the German scholar Joachim Camerarius (1500-1574), the Culdees founded a religious establishment at Pittenweem which was presided over by an abbot named Fillan. Many chroniclers have sought to identify this Fillan with St Fillan, an Irish saint of the seventh or eighth century (depending on which book one reads!). Camerarius would have had access to documents destroyed at the time of the Reformation, and his identification of Fillan as a Culdee preacher has the ring of truth about it.

Malcolm III (1058-1093) and his wife St Margaret suppressed most of the old forms of Christianity in Scotland and replaced them with the Church of Rome, but spared the Culdees out of respect for their piety and devotion. David I (1124-1153) was the fourth of Malcolm's sons to rule after him and had no such regard for the order. He systematically stripped them of all their possessions, and bestowed the manor of Pittenweem upon the monks of the May Island. It is possible that the confusion over the identity of St Fillan arose out of an attempt to obliterate Culdee influence from history after the order was disbanded.

In 1318 the Priory of the May with Pittenweem was granted to the Augustinian canons of St Andrews. After repeated English raids the island monastery was abandoned, and its occupants are thought to have moved to Pittenweem around the same date as the St Andrews charter was granted. In 1452 James II ratified all previous grants made to the church of St Andrews, which included the priory lands of Pittenweem and the Isle of May, listed as 'Pittenweem, Little Anstruther [now Anstruther Wester], Fawside, Lingo, Grangebriggs [Cairnbriggs] and Grangemuir'.

In 1540 John Rowle, Prior, received a charter from James V which stated that the Priory of Pittenweem was of small importance, with revenues largely derived from 'the labours of poor fishers', and added that the king wished to see the foundation expanded and the number of monks increased. Rowle was the last prior and was described by several of his contemporaries as a 'vile sensualist' (i.e. someone who was materialistic and devoid of spiritual life). As the storm-clouds of the Reformation loomed, he feued most of the priory lands to powerful neighbouring proprietors in an attempt to buy allies. In 1543 William Dishington of ⸻gemuir in which he was reminded ⸻ed on him. The charter also express⸻ ⸻ come to the defence of the institution 'when I ⸻ ⸻esies are budding forth on all sides'. The Reformation, however, was an unstoppable force and the Catholic Church was suppressed and all its possessions forfeited in 1559. The former priory and associated lands subsequently passed through the hands of several wealthy proprietors, styled 'commendators', and was erected into a temporal lordship in 1588 whilst under the ownership of William Stewart of Houston. In essence this meant that the church had no further claim on Pittenweem. It was created an independent parish in the same year.

The town itself must have been of some importance at an early date and its harbour is mentioned in the reign of William the Lion (1165-1214), when it is described as frequented by 'ships with four hawsers' and 'boats with fixed helms'. Pittenweem was created a free burgh by James III (1460-1488) and this status was reiterated by James V in a charter of confirmation in 1521, the original document having been lost. In 1540 the same monarch elevated the town to the status of a burgh of barony and just one year later conferred the title of royal burgh upon Pittenweem. Prior John Rowle granted the inhabitants the right to elect a provost and bailies, to hold a court house and create burgesses in 1547. The people of Pittenweem were also authorised to hold to weekly markets, on Sunday and Monday, and two annual fairs on the days of St Adrian the Martyr (4 March) and St Mary Magdalene (22 July). The prior also granted the burgh all adjacent 'moors and mosses' and the harbour, with all customs and duties pertaining to it.

The ports of the Fife coast enjoyed a flourishing trade with Europe during the sixteenth century, and this reached its peak around 1580. Ships arriving at Pittenweem brought cargoes of silk, wine and timber and returned to the Baltic and other countries with salt, malt, white fish and herring. In 1633 Pittenweem was described as 'very populous' and had 'ane guid safe harberie', built at the expense of the inhabitants. In 1638, however, thousands of people gathered at Greyfriars Church in Edinburgh to swear allegiance to the Solemn League and Covenant, protesting over Charles I's so-called 'reforms' of the Scottish church. Pittenweem rallied to this cause and forts were hurriedly erected for the burgh's defence. Scotland was plunged into a bloody war which culminated in the crushing of the Covenanting army at Kilsyth in 1645. The battle left 49 widows and 130 fatherless children in Pittenweem and the masters and entire crews of six merchant vessels belonging to the town were slain. Its fishing boats lay useless on the beach for want of men to sail them, and to add to the wretchedness of the place the town was stricken with plague. Civil war raged simultaneously with the Wars of the Covenant, and this placed an even heavier burden on Pittenweem. By 1656 only two ships of around 180 tons belonged to the burgh, compared to eight or ten at the outbreak of war. Further hardship was caused by a very poor herring fishery in the Forth from 1657 to 1693. In 1691 it was reported that Pittenweem could boast no foreign or inland trade, still had only two ships, and that these were mainly employed by Edinburgh merchants. Most of the houses in the burgh were ruinous, and many of those that were in repair were standing empty, although at the time the town did possess a small ketch of 55 tons and six small fishing boats.

The eighteenth century opens with one of the grimmest events in the annals of the burgh. In 1705 one Janet Cornfoot stood accused of witchcraft and fell into the hands of the mob. She was bound and beaten mercilessly, then dragged through the town and along the shore by her heels. The crowd was dispersed by a bailie, but quickly reassembled and tied the alleged witch from a rope stretched between a ship and the shore, swinging her to and fro and pelting her with stones. Bored with this, her tormentors cut the rope and she fell hard onto the shore, where she was again savagely beaten. She was tortured for three hours before being deliberately crushed to death under a door. The people of Pittenweem subsequently blamed this gruesome murder on a number of Englishmen and Orcadians who were in the town at the time, and no one was ever charged in connection with the crime.

Some of the earliest details of the fishing industry in Pittenweem are recorded by the historian Sibbald in 1710, who notes that six boats, each with a crew of six, were engaged in the white fishing and another fifteen boats with seven man crews took part in the summer herring fishery. In 1791 fish had become very scarce, but Pittenweem exported a considerable quantity of lobsters to customers in London. A flourishing kelp industry was also in existence at this time. The seaweed was burned in pits to create a mineral-rich ash which was a valuable fertiliser. Eight tons per annum were being produced in 1791, but the industry was abandoned before 1845.

It is believed that coal has been worked in the vicinity of Pittenweem since before the Reformation. In the late sixteenth century the right to work the Pittenweem coals was divided between James Balfour, Prior of Charterhouse, and Patrick Balfour of Pitcullo. Both of these had two salt pans which were supplied with coal from their pits. The rights to these pits and salt pans were acquired by William Stewart in 1594 and the salt pans were still noted in a charter of 1624, but were no longer operational by 1715. The Pittenweem coalfield straddles the parish boundary between Pittenweem and St Monans, and in 1771 Sir John Anstruther opened up new workings drained by a steam engine. Some of this coal was used to fuel his St Philip's Saltworks at St Monans, and he built a waggonway from the pits to Pittenweem. There he paid for improvements to be carried out to the East Pier to make it more suitable for the export of his coal and salt. The mines and saltworks were abandoned in 1823. Coal was briefly worked at Grangemuir, where the Walter Pit was sunk in 1902, but this was closed before 1907.

In 1755 Pittenweem had a population of 939; this had risen to 1,137 by 1791. A ten year slump in the fishing industry saw this number fall to 1,072 by 1801. The fishing recovered, and by 1861 the town had 1,710 inhabitants. Six years earlier it had 37 boats over 30 foot keel and thirteen smaller boats, employing over 200 men and boys. By 1881 it had a fleet of 91 boats, crewed by 240 fishermen, and the population of the town reached a peak of 1,991 in 1891. Boat numbers fell as larger vessels began to be employed on longer, more perilous voyages, and in 1904 Pittenweem had only 66 boats, but these gave work to 227 resident fishermen and 87 from other places.

Pittenweem's fleet consistently ranked third among the ports of Fife after Anstruther and St Monans. Following the First World War the town's fishermen became less involved in the herring fishery and many turned their attention to line fishing for haddock in local waters. By 1928 Pittenweem had 15 big boats, comprising 6 steam drifters and 9 motor boats, plus 21 motor boats under 30 foot keel and 5 small sail boats. These employed over 200 men and in that year Pittenweem landed the largest quantity of white fish of a Fife port (although the town's population had fallen to 1,644 by 1931).

The local winter herring fishery peaked in 1936, after which it went into a rapid decline as the shoals deserted the firth. The effects of this on the economies of Anstruther and St Monans was disastrous, but were felt less acutely in Pittenweem where white fish had become the fleet's staple source of income. The winter herring fishing was effectively abandoned in 1947 and in 1948 the value of fish landed at Pittenweem was the highest in Fife for the first time.

Today, little is now landed at Anstruther or St Monans and Pittenweem is the hub of the fishing industry on the Forth. The local fleet numbers some 20 large vessels, including three pair teams (comprising two vessels who fish one net together). These generally fish for white fish, although occasionally trawl for prawns. About 10 smaller boats usually fish for Nephrops (Norway prawns). Activity increases during the summer as Nephrop trawlers from the north-east of England, Arbroath and the west of Scotland congregate at Pittenweem. In a good year as many as 50 vessels have landed at Pittenweem.

Pittenweem is an architectural showpiece and its busy harbour renders it all the more attractive to the summer visitors who have become so vital to the economy of the East Neuk. It can still boast a diverse number of shops, plus banking and health facilities and six thriving fish merchants' businesses. Although opportunities for the young are limited, as in most rural areas, Pittenweem looks to have a healthier future ahead of it than many fishing towns.

Old PITTENWEEM

by
Eric Eunson

Pittenweem's burgh arms were blazoned by the Lyon King at Arms in 1676. The central figure represents St Adrian, who is said to have founded the monastic settlement on the Isle of May, the predecessor of the Augustinian Priory of Pittenweem. He is said to have been murdered along with his followers by Viking raiders in AD 874. In 1995 archaeologists uncovered a number of skeletons on the May. These are of a similar date to the saint's supposed murder and bear the marks of a violent death, thereby giving substance to early chronicles of the event.

© Eric Eunson 1999
First published in the United Kingdom, 1999,
by Stenlake Publishing, Ochiltree Sawmill, The Lade,
Ochiltree, Ayrshire, KA18 2NX
Telephone / Fax: 01290 423114

ISBN 1 84033 071 6

SELECT BIBLIOGRAPHY

Gifford, John, *The Buildings of Scotland, Fife*, 1988
Hay Fleming, D., *Guide to the East of Fife*, 1886
Pride, Glen, *The Kingdom of Fife, An Illustrated Architectural Guide*, 1990
Russell, C. S., *The East Fife Observer, 1914-1939*
Silver, Owen, *The Roads of Fife*, 1987
Smith, Peter, *The Lammas Drave and the Winter Herring*, 1985
Smith, Peter, *A History of Steam and the East Fife Fishing Fleet*, 1998
Wood, Walter, *The East Neuk of Fife*, 1887

Statistical Accounts, Pittenweem parish entries
dated 1790-1791, 1845 and 1951.

ACKNOWLEDGEMENTS

I would like to thank James Robertson of Lower Largo
for supplying me with information relating to William Fulton the boatbuilder.
Thanks to W. A. C. Smith for providing the picture on page 47.

BATHING POOL, PITTENWEEM.   A.748.

The natural reservoir created by the geology of the foreshore at the West Braes was in use as a public bathing pond by the end of the nineteenth century. In 1935, the date of this photograph, the town council carried out a number of improvements which included surrounding the pool with a concrete wall and erecting changing rooms, an attendant's pavilion, a three-tier diving board and a slide. Following a decline in the popularity of the pool it was closed, and the buildings have since been removed.

FECHNEY BAND PITTENWEEM

In August 1913 Pittenweem played host to 300 boys from the Fechnie Industrial School in Perth. They came in two parties of 150, each of which stayed for two weeks in the Mission Hall in Abbey Road. The second contingent arrived on Monday 17 August and marched from the station to their summer quarters accompanied by the strains of the school band, which had recently won the Oak Shield at the national Review of Boy Scouts.

Treat to Fechnie Boys Pittenweem

Every morning the Fechnie boys took a morning dip in the bathing pool and regularly entertained onlookers with life-saving demonstrations. This picture and the one opposite were taken by St Monans photographer William Easton on 21 August 1913, when the band played to a large crowd assembled on the West Braes, under the command of Captain H. Wadsworth. Locals supplied the boys with tea and biscuits before the band proceeded to the Market Place where a further concert was followed by a parade through the town.

Well into the 1950s the Braes and bathing pool were the venue for many local festivities. Victoria Day, Coronation sports, Sunday school picnics, and performances by the town band were just a few of the diversions on offer. Today it is the harbour which is the focus for the town in carnival mood, and the ever-popular Fishermen's Gala attracts large crowds every year. The Braes, meanwhile, have become the resort of walkers enjoying the Fife Coastal Path. I have been unable to identify this well-dressed gathering, photographed a year or two before the First World War, and would welcome information from any reader who recognises the event.

Pittenweem from the West

The houses at West Shore mostly date from the eighteenth century and the street has scarcely altered since this view was taken in the early 1920s. The extensive buildings to the rear of the houses were a cooperage, which was established in the 1880s at the peak of the local winter herring fishery. This closed before 1940 and following the removal of the buildings the site remained vacant until it was developed with houses in 1998. Pittenweem's gasworks stood just out of shot to the left. It was established in 1831 and remained independent until 1936 when it merged with the St Andrews Gas Company. Although electricity was introduced to the burgh in 1934, gas was still used to light the streets until the 1950s.

West Shore, Pittenweem.

73293. J.V.

Mending the nets at West Shore in 1909. Although the presence of a woman on a fishing boat would have been unthinkable (because of the bad luck superstition said she would bring), fishermen's wives and daughters performed most of the onshore tasks associated with the industry, mending nets, baiting hooks, gutting herring and knitting most of their menfolk's sea clothes. Little wonder that a girl from a non-fishing family marrying into a fishing one was pitied by her relations – as indeed her husband was by his.

West Harbour, Pittenweem

This picture postcard of the House on the Rock was published in 1905, but the negative number dates the photograph to 1893. The house on the far left was abandoned after it was damaged by storms on 17 and 18 October 1898, said to be the worst the area had experienced for sixty years. It remained empty until the 1920s, when it was incorporated into a remodelling of the adjacent property (which now goes by the name Rockvilla). In the foreground is the head of the West or Boat Harbour, which was formerly used by small fishing craft in good weather. The natural rock skerry which protected this anchorage was modified with masonry in 1848 to create a low-water pier for the convenience of passengers travelling on paddle steamers belonging to the Anstruther and Leith Steam Packet Company.

An unusual 1904 view of Mid Shore and the West Pier. The West Pier was built in 1724 by William Aitken after consultation with William Adam of Kirkcaldy, the father of the famous brothers John and Robert Adam, who designed many of Britain's best-known Georgian buildings. The pier was completely rebuilt in 1822 and in 1872 was extended eastward to enclose the West Basin of the harbour, which was deepened at the same time. The debt for these works was not cleared by the town until 1930. The tip of the pier was widened during harbour improvements in 1951.

Freshly tarred drift net buoys, known locally as 'pallats' or 'boughs', indicate that this 1910 view was taken as the herring fleet was making ready to sail. The building on the extreme left was built in 1888 but incorporates a date-stone of 1624 from the property it replaced. Further along the street, three blocks east of the foot of Water Wynd, is an imposing merchant's house with a curvilinear chimney gable to the sea. This is a feature characteristic of Scottish Renaissance architecture of the seventeenth century. The house was almost totally rebuilt in 1972 and its sharp-edged window and door surrounds have still to weather convincingly.

Many ancient properties in Mid Shore and East Shore were rebuilt between 1870 and 1890 during a peak in the local herring fishery. This turn of the century view shows some of the last to be replaced, at the foot of Water Wynd and to the right of the seventeenth century house with the curved gable. When they were demolished in 1904 the local paper reported that the oldest of them dated back to 1620. The East Pier, in the right foreground, is the oldest part of the harbour and was probably first built during the second half of the sixteenth century. It was extended by George Cowie and Alexander Gilbert in 1641, but was destroyed by a storm in 1655 and remained ruinous until it was rebuilt by Thomas Coventry in 1688. It was again damaged and repaired in 1702 and 1723, and major repairs and improvements were made in 1771 by Sir John Anstruther for the shipment of his coal and salt from St Monans.

This picture shows the buildings at the foot of Water Wynd that were removed in 1904 in closer detail. In the 1880s a house stood on the west side of this wynd which had belonged to a Mr Archibald Douglas in the early eighteenth century. His son John (1721-1807) was a prolific writer of political pamphlets; from 1787 to 1791 he was Bishop of Carlisle, and Bishop of Salisbury from 1791 until his death. Douglas's house was separated from the street by a courtyard and was lined with carved oak panelling. This fine old building was removed before 1900.

This 1906 picture of Mid Shore shows three vessels under construction at William Fulton's boatyard beside the granary. Fulton was born in St Monans in 1846, and upon leaving school served a four year apprenticeship with a boatbuilder in the town, followed by another three years in a Glasgow shipyard. He came to Pittenweem in the late 1860s, where he earned a scant living repairing boats. An elderly baker befriended the hard-working lad and bought him the house on the west corner of Mid Shore and Water Wynd. William turned the garden to the rear into a workshop for building boats, and converted part of the house into a provision store and ship's chandlery.

Just as William Fulton was consolidating his new business, his wife died leaving him to care for eight children. Shortly after, the local bank agent absconded with all his cash, and a slump in the herring fishery left him with a string of bad debts. He managed to save his business, but always said that these catastrophes had taken a toll on his health. Fulton is the bearded gentleman third from the left in the front row in this 1890s picture. His son John sits at the right hand end of the front row, with his brother Christopher sitting on his right, and a third brother Jim, standing between them. The larger Fifie boats built by Fulton, and five steam drifters (two built in 1892, two in 1895 and one in 1906), were launched broadside into the harbour as the yard did not have access to a slipway for a conventional launch.

GUTTING. PITTENWEEM

Women and girls gutting herring at the harbourhead in 1907. Fresh herring are highly perishable and need to be gutted within hours of being caught. Most of the herring caught in Scotland which were not consumed locally were cured in salt and exported to markets in Germany, Russia and Eastern Europe. The gutters worked in teams of three, two gutters and a packer, and an experienced gutter could prepare thirty fish a minute. The troughs where the job was performed were known as farlans. In 1855 there were 43 coopers, 16 curers and 407 gutters at Pittenweem. Since these numbers were disproportionate to the needs of the town's fleet, it is likely that it was used as a herring station by boats from other ports. The gutting girls were last seen at work in Pittenweem in the 1920s, but by 1928 very little herring was caught by Pittenweem boats.

Fish Market, Pittenweem.

A sea of flat caps dominates this early 1930s view of Pittenweem fish-market at the West Pier. The fish-market was relocated to a covered site on the east side of the granary in 1954, which was replaced a few years ago during a major refurbishment of the whole of the harbourhead. Today Pittenweem has the only fish-market in the East of Fife area, and in 1973 the Fishery Board transferred its fishery officer to Pittenweem from Anstruther, where the industry had reached the last stages of a terminal decline. Pittenweem now has the only fishery officer between Alloa and the Tay.

Landing the Catch, Pittenweem.

Two traditional 'bauldies' belonging to Pittenweem are moored side by side next to the pier in this early 1930s photograph. The one nearest the pier is the *Volunteer* and her neighbour is the *Launch Out*. The other two boats are canoe-sterned 'nabbies'; LH165 is the *Robina Inglis* of Newhaven and KY59 is the *Courageous II* of Pittenweem. In 1922 the first vessel of this type was built at St Monans for a Campbeltown skipper who intended to use her for ring netting. Around 1930 nabbies became popular with fishermen in Pittenweem and, to a lesser extent, St Monans. Pittenweem adopted the use of ring nets in 1936 and its fleet was subsequently dominated by this class of boat until the 1960s.

The granary at the harbour was built around 1800 (no published source provides an accurate date for its construction). This picture of the harbour was taken in 1904 when extensive improvements, begun in the previous year, were nearing completion – note the cranes on the right. The most significant of these improvements was the construction of the South Pier, which several current books wrongly describe as Victorian. A concrete extension of the South Pier beyond the lighthouse was carried out by the contractor Robert Terras of East Wemyss in 1951.

The Harbour. Pittenweem

The steam drifter leaving port in this late 1920s postcard view is the *Restless Wave*, owned by Robert Hughes of Pittenweem. Steam fishing boats became popular with Anstermen during the 1890s, but it wasn't until 1906 that one appeared in Pittenweem. She was the 90 foot *Preston*, KY121, built by William Fulton for her skipper George Horsburgh who owned her until the 1930s. In 1914 the East Neuk fleet contained its largest number of steam drifters, 64 in all, most of which belonged to Anstruther. At this date Pittenweem had nine, but by 1928 this number had fallen to six and the town's last steam drifter disappears from records in 1937.

"A Stormy Day", Pittenweem Harbour. 15

The bauldies in this late 1930s view have their gear on board for drift netting, but are confined to harbour by heavy seas. Pittenweem Harbour is difficult to enter when the wind blows hard from the east as a broadside sea breaks over the pier and there is a heavy run in the harbour itself. Bauldies were popular on both sides of the Forth from around 1880 to 1900, although they remained a significant part of the Pittenweem fleet until after the Second World War. Named inexplicably after the Italian patriot Garibaldi, they were generally under thirty foot keel and were smaller cousins of Fifies, which were also characterised by straight bow and stern posts.

An early picture of the Gyles, dating from before 1900. The two-storey corner building was remodelled and the old houses to the rear in Abbey Wall Road were removed at around this time. Gyles House at the head of the South Pier dates from 1626 and was once the home of Captain James Cook, who carried Charles II to Holland aboard his Pittenweem brig the *Surprise* after the king's defeat at Worcester in 1651. Cook later renamed the vessel *Royal Escape*. The tall house with the chimney on the front was rebuilt in the late seventeenth century, but incorporates part of a building dating from 1597.

THE HARBOUR, PITTENWEEM.

A.745

The harbour and Gyles, photographed from the tip of the West Pier in 1934. The crane on the pier was used to lower the booms visible in the picture into the water to close the harbour mouth during easterly gales, and from 1906 until the late 1940s all the big Pittenweem boats at the winter herring fished out of Anstruther. The crane and booms were removed after the extension of the South Pier in 1951 made the harbour mouth safer. The bauldies at the pier were probably engaged in 'sma' lining' – inshore line fishing for haddock. Pittenweem was the last East Neuk port to employ this fishing method and persisted into the 1950s. The mussels which were used for bait were brought from the Eden estuary.

The Gyles were the subject of a major restoration by the National Trust for Scotland which began in 1962. Plans were drawn up by the Kirkcaldy architects Wheeler and Sproson and the joinery work was by Freddie Horne of Lower Largo. Today the Gyles are a popular subject for artists and photographers, although they are now denied the perspective of this 1904 picture by a high wall adjoining a house in Abbey Wall Road.

The pend through the house on the left of this 1920s view of Abbey Wall Road led to Welch Brothers' Abbey Park sawmills and fish-curing premises. Between the wars they advertised a charabanc which could be hired by touring parties to view the district. The houses further up the street were part of the first council housing scheme in the burgh, named Abbey Park and completed in 1922. Glebe Park, on the opposite side of the street, was built during a second phase in 1930.

St Fillan's Cave, from which Pittenweem derives its name, consists of two chambers linked to the garden of the priory by a passageway. The passage had collapsed before the end of the eighteenth century and was forgotten until its accidental rediscovery by the Rev. J. Crabbe around 1860. A one-time haunt of smugglers, the cave was latterly used as a store by fishermen. It was cleared out and restored in 1935 by Robert Williamson of Pittenweem, under the supervision of the Episcopal Church rector, Rev. Walter H. De Voil. The shrine was rededicated on 21 September 1935, and two years later the cave was lit by electricity.

THE PRIOR'S LODGING, PITTENWEEM PRIORY, NOW ST. JOHN'S RECTORY   A.9889

The Prior's Lodging is the only building on the south side of the priory quadrangle to remain. It was once flanked to the east by either an extension of the same house or a separate dwelling, and in 1699 this was inhabited by Dr Andrew Bruce, Bishop of Dunkeld. The fifteenth century vaulted ground floor is the oldest part of the lodging; the upper floors date mainly from the sixteenth and early seventeenth centuries. The dormer windows and projecting bay (on the right of this 1947 picture) are thought to date from its conversion into the Episcopalian Church manse in the 1840s.

THE 15ᵗʰ CENTURY GATE HOUSE, PITTENWEEM PRIORY.
A. 9891.

This fifteenth century gateway with a porter's lodge on the first floor is reckoned to be the oldest surviving part of the priory complex, and once led to an 'inner close' or paved courtyard. The remains of a stair to the rear led to a walkway which ran along the top of the high wall that enclosed the quadrangle; this was described as being wide enough to walk along two-abreast. Several women were burned for witchcraft at the foot of this stair in 1643 and 1644, and their menfolk were forced to meet the cost of their wives' executions!

The leftmost part of the building in this Edwardian photograph once housed the chapter chamber and vestries of the priory, and the monks' dormitory. In 1588 it became the Parish Church manse. It was later the home of Bailie Gavin Hogg, factor to the Anstruthers of Balcaskie. He allowed the first floor be used by the Episcopalians as a meeting place, but the top floor was let to the Anstruthers as a granary. This attracted such a profusion of rats that the Episcopalians were forced to vacate to a house in the High Street! A huge growth of ivy to the rear threatened the structure's survival, but this was removed when Sir Robert Lorimer restored the building in 1921. The adjoining part of the building, formerly the monks refectory, had its front wall and gable rebuilt when it became the town hall in 1821. Another building further to the right was once styled Bishop Bruce's Library, but no substantial remnants of this survive.

Marygate and nearby Lady Wynd derive their names from the Lady Chapel. This was one of the priory buildings and stood partly on the north-west corner of the churchyard. It was demolished around 1865 to allow the road to be straightened. A square fortified tower, set within the north-east corner of the priory wall, stood at the opposite end of Marygate. This contained a stair which led to an arch across the street which was the East Port of the burgh. During the early nineteenth century armed men were stationed on this tower to keep watch for resurrectionists (body snatchers). The buildings on the left of this 1893 picture were among five houses and two ruins in Marygate that were condemned by the town council in 1932.

Another view of the condemned sixteenth century houses in Marygate, demolished in 1933. A plaque on a nearby wall states that in 1736 Andrew Wilson of Pathhead and George Robertson relieved James Stark, a Kirkcaldy customs man of £200 (the proceeds from a sale of seized contraband at Anstruther) in an inn at this end of the street. The men were caught, tried and sentenced to hang in Edinburgh. But public sympathy was with them and when Wilson attacked his guards and bade Geordie Robertson flee, the crowd did not hinder his escape. One Captain Porteous of the City Guard ordered his men to fire on the crowd and several were killed. Porteous was sentenced to hang on 8 September 1736, but received a six week reprieve. He was dragged from his cell the night after his stay of execution and lynched by a large mob, not one of whom was ever apprehended!

A turn of the century view looking east from the Parish Church tower. The open land in the background is now filled with modern housing, including Abbey Park (1922) and Priory Court (1971). The Episcopal Church of St John the Evangelist (foreground) was built in 1805, and was the fourth and final place of worship that the town's Episcopalian congregation occupied in a century. This dignified little Gothic box became T-shaped when an east sanctuary was added in 1869-1870. The north porch onto Marygate was added at the same time.

There was no place of public worship in Pittenweem prior to the erection of the burgh and its associated lands into a parish in 1588. The nearest kirk was in Anstruther Wester, which was disjoined from Pittenweem and created into a parish in its own right in the same year. Pittenweem Parish Church was adapted from one of the old priory buildings, possibly a granary, shortly after these events took place. The adjoining tower was also built in 1588 as the burgh tollbooth, and contained a prison on the ground floor and a council chamber above. Its projecting fifth storey and spire were added in the early seventeenth century, and contain two bells dated 1663 and 1742. The town clock was made in 1773 by Pittenweem clockmaker John Smith.

The building that was converted into the church was long thought to date from 1532, the year inscribed on a stone built into the south wall. However, in 1981 the church was stripped of its harling during a major refurbishment, giving archaeologists the opportunity to carry out a detailed survey. A fragment of a doorway identified as dating from c.1200 was uncovered near the east end of the north wall, making it the oldest building on the priory site. It is thought that the building originally extended further east than does the present church. Pittenweem was granted to the monks of the May between 1124 and 1152, suggesting that they had a chapel here which may have occupied the site of an earlier Culdee foundation. The north entrance to the church, on the left of this 1905 view, was built in 1882 and designed by Pittenweem's session clerk, James Brown.

Three-quarters of a century has wrought few major changes to this atmospheric view of the High Street, dating from the early 1920s. The premises in the right foreground were then occupied by Archibald Tosh, wine and spirit merchant and Italian warehouseman, but have since been converted into a private home. The foundations of walls were visible in gardens further east on this side of the street in the 1880s. These were the remains of the lazaretto of the priory, a building which stood outwith the walls of the priory and would have been used by the monks to treat the diseased poor, particularly lepers. The priory site has many secrets to yield, and would make a fascinating subject for Channel 4's 'Time Team'!

Kellie Lodging was built in the late sixteenth century as a town house for the Earls of Kellie, but by 1651 it was occupied by Robert Smith, the town clerk of Pittenweem. In the spring of that year Charles II made a progress through Fife, rallying the support of county lairds to join the Scottish army he was raising to continue his fight against Cromwell. With the king's arrival at Pittenweem expected, the bailies and council ordered the town's colours to be hoisted on the bartizan (balustrade) of the steeple, and decreed that the bells should be rung from three o'clock until the king had left the burgh. Mr George Hamilton, the minister, and the bailies and council (dressed in their best apparel) waited for Charles at the West Port, a gateway to the burgh which stood at the west end of the High Street. With them was a guard of 'twenty four of the ablest men, with partizans [pikes]', and another twenty-four armed with muskets. The party conveyed the king and his retinue to Robert Smith's house, where a table was set, covered with one of Lord Kellie's finest carpets. The Pittenweem baker George Hedderwick had prepared 'some great buns, and other wheat bread of the finest order, baken with sugar, cannell and other spices fitting', and James Richardson and Walter Airth provided 'eight or ten gallons of good strong ale, with canary, sack, Rhenish wine, tent, white and claret wines, that his Majesty and his court might eat and drink'. As Charles II departed Pittenweem, after what sounds like a right royal booze-up, a signal was given to Andrew Tod at the steeple-head, who in turn signalled the town's thirty-six cannon to fire a salute to the king. This picture of the Kellie Lodging was taken by Charles F. S. Burrows of Anstruther in the early 1920s. When the lodging was restored in 1969 the adjoining single-storey shop was removed. I doubt whether the Environmental Health Department would allow the combination of hairdressing and ice-cream parlour today.

Pittenweem High Street was not always a commercial thoroughfare, and in the seventeenth century contained the town houses of several country lairds. The building entered by the second doorway from the left in this 1910 photograph was built in the seventeenth century for the Arnots of Balcormo (Balcormo being an estate just north-west of Balcaskie House). The Episcopalians met in a room on the first floor of this house after they took flight from Bailie Hogg's rats in the priory. The white house beyond it carries a date-stone of 1635, but was rebuilt around 1720 when it was in use as the Parish Church manse. The original property on the site had belonged to the Abercrombies of Abercrombie, who flourished between the twelfth and the seventeenth centuries.

High Street, Pittenweem

When this 1909 picture was taken Pittenweem post office was owned by A. A. Henderson. The earliest record of a post office in the burgh is dated 1740. In 1898 the building with the elaborately-painted gable end was owned by Alexander Wilkie, ironmonger and grocer. The business was established in 1816, and around 1900 Wilkie was succeeded by E. Birrell, who advertised himself as a grocer, ironmonger, china merchant and boot and shoe factor, adding that 'tennis requisites are a speciality'. He was followed by his son James Birrell, but on 9 April 1932 'Birrell's Emporium' was completely gutted by fire. The building was demolished and its site taken by new premises built for Henry Lawson, joiner and picture-frame maker. Lawson was the inventor of a successful mitreing machine.

PITTENWEEM CYCLE PARADE

On the evening of Wednesday 29 July 1913 a fancy dress cycle parade through Pittenweem took place, organised by the town council 'for the purpose of enlivening the burgh during the Fair'. This photograph was taken by William Easton and shows part of the record crowd which assembled outside the South School in Routine Row to witness the start of the event. The South School, on the left, was built in the 1870s to provide additional school accommodation following the passing of the 1872 Education Act (Scotland), which made schooling compulsory for every child from five to thirteen. It was closed in 1913 and converted into a cinema by A. B. McNair in 1921. When this closed in the 1960s the building became home to the town's Boy Scout troop.

The 1913 cycle parade attracted eighteen entries, each of whom paid a threepenny entry fee. They cycled to Elie and back before reassembling outside the South School for judging. Provost Smart and Bailie Nicholson awarded first prize to Mr P. Boyle, right, for what appears to be a mountie costume. He was presented with a handsome silver badge made by Robert Jack, jeweller. The corner building in the background presently houses the business of C. P. Bowman, fish merchant.

A series of entertainments followed the 1913 cycle parade, including a dance in the Market Place with music provided by Robert Hughes' band. This group of blacked-up performers staged humorous sketches in the grounds of the old priory.

Although many of the houses in South Loan have been modernised, a couple of them a bit heavy-handedly, the street has changed little since this 1911 postcard was sent. The photograph was taken by A. Mungall, Pittenweem's chemist. The junction on the right leads into Routine Row, which derives its name from following the course of the routine or processional route of the Augustinian monks of the priory. Latterly this was corrupted into Rottenrow, but in recent years its old name has been reinstated.

Not the best of photographs, but this may be the only surviving illustration of the former Infant School in James Street, which stood on the west side of the present school entrance. I have been unable to date the building, but from its multi-paned, Gothic arched windows, would judge it to be contemporary with the primary schools at Crail (dating from 1822, and now the public library) and Kingsbarns (1824), which exhibit the same feature. By 1880 Pittenweem had three schools; this one, the South School in Routine Row, and the North School, which stood on the site of the present Pittenweem Primary School, built in 1913. The old Infant School was demolished in July the same year.

Milton Place, Pittenweem.

79075 JV.

The villas in Milton Place were all brand spanking new when this photograph was taken in 1910; twenty years later the council houses on the opposite side of the road robbed them of their sea views. Behind the trees on the right is the entrance to Christ the King Roman Catholic Church, converted in 1935 from a Georgian villa dating from *c*.1830. Above the porch entrance is a statue of Our Lord robed against the Cross, carved by Sir Hew Lorimer in 1952. Another sculpture by Lorimer, of St Joseph with the child Christ holding a saw, is to be found inside.

JV 73299

In 1857 there were just a couple of houses on the east side of Charles Street at its junction with James Street. On the west side it was built up as far as the present Anchor Inn, which was originally a villa of around 1830 called Pittenweem Lodge. This was later converted into the Station Hotel. The street developed to its present proportions during the second half of the nineteenth century. This illustration dates from 1910.

Pittenweem station lay about half a mile north of the town, beyond the end of Charles Street. It opened on 1 September 1863 as part of the Leven and East Fife Railway's extension from Kilconquhar, which had been the terminus since 1857, to Anstruther. Owing to a manpower shortage the station was closed to all traffic on 1 January 1917. The North British Railway Company's decision to make this closure was challenged by the town council, who pointed out that the NBR were in breach of an agreement of 1861 made when the land was sold to the L&EFR. This contained the condition that all normal trains would stop at Pittenweem. A concession was made that from 14 April 1917 certain goods trains would stop at the station, but passenger services were not reinstated until after the war. This photograph was taken on 4 September 1965, two days before the Leven to St Andrews line was axed.

In 1534 Prior John Rowle feued Easter Grangemuir to George Borthwick and in 1543 Wester Grangemuir was granted to William Dishington of Ardross. In the late eighteenth century both portions were bought by Thomas Bruce, who is listed as being a director of the Hercules Insurance Company in 1815. He built the first part of the mansion in this 1905 view in 1807. The bay window and eastern extension which disturb its classical symmetry were added in 1830. Grangemuir replaced an earlier house which stood about 200 yards to the south and was said to be haunted by a ghost. This spectre went by the name of 'Baff Barefoot' and manifested itself solely in the sound of unshod feet running through the rooms of the house. It is said that no stones from the old building were used in the new house in case the ghost was brought with them! Since 1974 Grangemuir House has been at the centre of a holiday chalet complex.